Eric Vanderburg

Critical factors contributing to a student's decision to pirat

I0003108

Der GRIN Verlag publiziert seit 1998 wissenschaftliche Arbeiten von Studenten, Hochschullehrern und anderen Akademikern als eBook und gedrucktes Buch. Die Verlagswebsite www.grin.com ist die ideale Plattform zur Veröffentlichung von Hausarbeiten, Abschlussarbeiten, wissenschaftlichen Aufsätzen, Dissertationen und Fachbüchern.

Document Nr. V203595

Eric Vanderburg

Critical factors contributing to a student's decision to pirate software

GRIN Verlag

Die Deutsche Bibliothek verzeichnet diese Publikation in der Deutschen Nationalbibliografie; detaillierte bibliografische Daten sind im Internet über http://dnb.d-nb.de/ abrufbar.

1. Auflage 2009
Copyright © 2009 GRIN Verlag GmbH
http://www.grin.com
Druck und Bindung: Books on Demand GmbH, Norderstedt Germany
ISBN 978-3-656-31083-9

Critical factors contributing to a student's decision to pirate software

JurInnov Research Report

Eric Vanderburg

June 24, 2009

Abstract

Research Report

by

Eric Vanderburg

June 24, 2009

The goal of this study was to analyze the factors contributing to a student's decision to pirate software. The study focused on students in computer technology disciplines. A quantitative approach was used to test the hypotheses of difficulty, impact, cost/value, risk, and right. The results of the study show that the moral attitudes of whether it is wrong to pirate software are present in those who do not copy software but absent in those who do. The research is valuable for practitioners and policy makers.

Table of Contents

List of Tables

List of Figures

Chapter 1
Rationale

1.1 Problem Statement

Software piracy is a threat to software developers and companies. It undermines their ability to make a profit on their work. This study asks the question, for what reasons do students choose whether to make illegal copies of software? The study collects data from three classrooms but the analysis does not factor in the course or other demographic variables when separating out responses.

1.2 Background/Introduction

Software piracy is often mentioned in the media but the reasons for why people copy software are largely unknown (Siponen and Vartiainen, 2007). Kin-wai Lau cites a 1990 study by Swinyard et al. where students in the US were found to have more respect for copyright laws than students in Singapore (2007). In support of this, Gan and Koh (2006) state that intellectual property rights have less value in Asian cultures. Marron and Steel (2000) found it to be inversely related to software piracy. Additionally, Depken and Simmons (2004) concluded that software piracy declines as income increases. Technological proficiency would be an important demographic variable studied previously by Gan and Koh in 2006. Gan and Koh's study found that those with 8-10 years of personal computer experience tended to pirate software seldom whereas those with 4 or less years experience with personal computers pirated often. Moral sensitivity would be an interesting demographic variable to use to see whether general ethical principles include software piracy or if it is still as Vitell and Davis stated in 1990, that software piracy has become socially acceptable because it is so commonplace. Gan and Koh (2006) conducted a study on software piracy in university students and faculty in Singapore in which a cluster analysis was used that divided respondents into categories based on variables including ethical attitudes.

This study builds on the work of Siponen and Vartiainen (2007), Gan and Koh (2006), Depken and Simmons (2004), Marron and Steel (2000), Kin-wai Lau (2007), and Vitell and Davis (1990) who studied software piracy and Akbulut (2008) who studied ethics between genders. The goal of this study was to analyze the factors contributing to

a student's decision to pirate software. The study focuses on students in computer technology disciplines.

1.3 Opportunity for Research

This research is useful for improving computer ethics education. The results of the study show that the moral attitudes of whether it is wrong to pirate software are present in those who do not copy software but absent in those who do. This is one area where computer ethics education can place more effort. Software piracy awareness campaigns could similarly benefit from the research.

1.4 Research Objective

The goal of this study was to analyze the factors contributing to a student's decision to pirate software. The study focused on students in computer technology disciplines.

1.5 Research Question(s)

Several questions are asked in this research study to answer the overall question of why students in computer technology programs decide to pirate software. The questions are as follows: Is the likelihood of a student choosing to pirate software independent of the perceived level of difficulty to pirate software? Question 2: Is the likelihood of a student choosing to pirate software independent of the perceived harm pirating software causes? Question 3: Is the likelihood of a student choosing to pirate software independent of the software cost? Question 4: Is the likelihood of a student choosing to pirate software independent of the threat of punishment? Question 5: Is the likelihood of a student choosing to pirate software independent of the perceived right to use the software without paying for it?

Chapter 2

Methodology

2.1 Theoretical Framework

This research builds upon the work of Siponen and Vartiainen's "Unauthorized copying of software – An empirical study of reasons for and against" (2007) where the factors influencing the Finnish students' decision to pirate software was studied.

Siponen and Vartiainen (2007) ask the question, for what reasons do students choose whether to make illegal copies of software? The study collects data from three classrooms but the analysis does not factor in the course or other demographic variables when separating out responses. The study is a non-experiment because the researchers did not have any control over independent variables.

An anonymous quantitative survey was used in the study. This promoted honesty in the responses which is especially important when discussing software piracy as it is a crime. The survey had a list of possible reasons for making illegal copies of software. The advantage of presenting respondents with a list of reasons is that the students are more likely to be able to choose a reason as compared to an open ended question that might result in many responses of "I don't know". The downside of listing possible reasons is that the respondents will be encouraged to choose the one that best matches their situation but it may not accurately reflect the reason they choose to illegally copy software. The survey also does not take into account multiple reasons for making illegal copies and the varying degree of influence each may have had on the student's decision to copy software because the students do not rank their answers and they select only one reason.

The goal of Siponen and Vartiainen's study was to better understand the reasons why Finnish students choose to make illegal copies of software. Their study found that the most common reason for pirating software is that software is expensive (2007). Some copied software because they could not afford it and other copied the software to save money.

2.1.1 Research Hypothesis / Questions

Five hypotheses have been postulated. They are as follows:

Hypothesis 1: The likelihood of a student choosing to pirate software is independent of the perceived level of difficulty.

Hypothesis 2: The likelihood of a student choosing to pirate software is independent of the perceived harm pirating software causes.

Hypothesis 3: The likelihood of a student choosing to pirate software is independent of the software cost.

Hypothesis 4: The likelihood of a student choosing to pirate software is independent of the threat of punishment.

Hypothesis 5: The likelihood of a student choosing to pirate software is independent of the perceived right to use the software without paying for it.

2.1.2 Operational Definitions of Variables

The study is a hypothesis test. The five hypotheses in section 2.1.1 will be used to answer the research question on a student's decision to pirate software.

2.2 Research Design Approach

The study is a hypothesis test to answer the question on what influences the decision of students in computer technology programs decide to pirate software.

2.3 Context of Study

The goal of this study is to analyze the factors contributing to a student's decision to pirate software. Because of this, an ideal location would be a college or university where students can be interviewed or surveyed easily. This study proposes to study students at a local college on the east side of Cleveland, Ohio. The location was chosen primarily because it is a school and the study focuses on students. A school is a good place to survey students because they spend a lot of time there. With the cooperation of the professors at the school, a better response rate can be achieved as well because the students are compelled to complete the survey in class. A secondary reason for choosing the site is because the researcher has a good working relationship with the professors there and they are willing to distribute the survey to their classes for him.

2.3.1 Setting

The location is college on the east side of Cleveland, Ohio. The location was chosen because the researcher is on the board there and the professors there are willing to distribute the survey to their classes. The college is a career college that offers associate of applied science degrees in computer technology, building maintenance technology, electrical technology, and environmental systems as well as several diploma programs. The school is located on the East side of Cleveland and the students are a mix of traditional and non-traditional. Traditional being those who attend directly after high school and non-traditional being those who attend in order to gain the skills to change careers.

2.3.2 Population

The population to be studied is students in information technology in the Cleveland metropolitan area of Ohio. The local College's computer technology program contains such students. The student body in these courses is made up of people from the Cleveland metropolitan area. The school is a small one with less than 20 students in the computer technology program so the population size is small. Students in the computer technology program were chosen because Siponen and Vartiainen's study found that half the students who said they found software piracy acceptable would be less inclined if they worked in the computer field (2007). The students surveyed are preparing to work in this field so it is useful to understand their opinions on the subject during their program prior to them working in the industry.

2.3.3 Limitations

The first constraint would be whether a minimum number of respondents would be necessary to perform an accurate statistical analysis. Another constraint could be the amount of time survey participants have to take the survey. A third constraint could be the possible lack of control that could happen when persons other than the researcher administer the quantitative survey in the classroom. These professors can be given training in the proper procedure for administering the survey but care must be taken to make sure that the surveys are administered professionally. Another constraint would be the way partial responses or incomplete responses are dealt with. Lastly, The College is a small school with less than 20 students in the computer technology program. This makes for a very small population and sample.

2.3.4 Sample Design and Selection

The students at the college are a mix of traditional and non-traditional. Traditional students are those who attend directly after high school and non-traditional students are those who attend in order to gain the skills to change careers. The population is made up primarily of male students. Only 10% of the 20 students are female. Age of the population ranges from 18 to 55. Some are single and others are married. Three ethnicities are represented in the school, Black, White, and Hispanic.

2.4 Feasibility Analysis and Design Selection

The variables were measured using a likert scale on a scale of 1 to 5 with a possible answer of strongly agree, agree, neutral, disagree, and strongly disagree.

The demographic variables were analyzed by computing the distribution across each category. Demographic variables include ethnicity, gender, income, financial aid, technical proficiency, student status, and risk tolerance. A quantitative approach was used to test the hypotheses of difficulty, impact, cost, risk, and right. The quantitative approach is used with the scaled variables. The Statistical Package for Social Science (SPSS) version 17 was used for hypothesis testing and to produce relevant demographic statistics.

Based on the dependent variable of whether or not the students pirate software, the responses were gathered into two groups. Each group was analyzed with a one-sample T test. The researcher used this test because the research has a sample size of 17 and the t-test is used on sample sizes less than 30. The t-test can be used to determine if the findings from the research can be applied to a larger population. Also the means of the response are used to determine the mean response and to make observations.

2.5 Data Collection

This section provides a description of the method used for measuring the variables, the instruments used, the collection procedures, how the data is coded, and how it was collected..

2.5.1 Methods of Measurement

The study defines the dependent variable as the likelihood of a student choosing to pirate software. The independent variables are (1) the perceived level of difficulty to pirate software (Weisband and Goodman, 1992), (2) the perceived harm pirating software causes (Stallman 1995, Weckert 1997), (3) software cost (Weisband and Goodman, 1992) and value (Takeyama 2002), (4) threat of punishment (Cheng et al. 1997), and (5) the perceived right to use software without paying for it. Each of these independent variables is a theoretical reason for software piracy. Siponen and Vartiainen's study uses some of these as well as the view of software as intangible, prevalence of piracy, and software quality (2007).

The responses will be scored between one and five (Likert Scale) based on how strongly the student agrees or disagrees with the statement. The scale of one to five matches with strongly disagree, disagree, neutral, agree, and strongly agree.

2.5.2 Instrumentation

The first three questions, "Copying software does not require a lot of technical skill", "It is simple to copy software", and "The process of copying software is quick" map to the first hypothesis, "The likelihood of a student choosing to pirate software is independent of the perceived level of difficulty". Technological proficiency is a variable studied previously by Gan and Koh in 2006. Gan and Koh's study found that those with 8-10 years of personal computer experience tended to pirate software seldom whereas those with 4 or less years experience with personal computers pirated often.

The fourth and fifth questions are "pirating software is harmless" and "software companies lose money when I pirate software". These questions maps to the second hypothesis, "The likelihood of a student choosing to pirate software is independent of the perceived harm pirating software causes".

The sixth and seventh survey questions are "Software is too expensive" and "Software is not worth the price companies charge for it". These questions map to the third hypothesis, "The likelihood of a student choosing to pirate software is independent of the software cost". Siponen & Vartiainen (2007) used a similar variable "software is expensive" in their study of on software piracy in Finnish students.

The eighth and ninth survey questions are "It is doubtful that I would be caught if I pirated software" and "Copyright protection laws are not often enforced". These

questions map to the fourth hypothesis, "The likelihood of a student choosing to pirate software is independent of the threat of punishment". In the study "Unauthorized Copying of Software – An Empirical Study of Reasons for and against", Siponen & Vartiainen (2007) used the variable "Although it is forbidden by law, the risk of getting caught is negligible" in their study of on software piracy in Finnish students.

The tenth, eleventh, and twelfth survey questions are "I have a right to use software without paying for it", "It is wrong to pirate software", and "Software is intangible and should not be paid for". These questions map to the fifth hypothesis, "The likelihood of a student choosing to pirate software is independent of the perceived right to use the software without paying for it". Moral sensitivity was a variable used to see whether general ethical principles include software piracy or if it is still as Vitell and Davis stated in 1990, that software piracy has become socially acceptable because it is so commonplace. Gan and Koh (2006) conducted a study on software piracy in university students and faculty in Singapore in which a cluster analysis was used that divided respondents into categories based on variables including ethical attitudes. In this case a person's ethical attitude was considered a valid variable to measure. According to Weckert, one moral reason for the copying of software is the view of software as intangible (1997).

The pilot questionnaire was revised to include several questions that map to each of the hypotheses because it was determined that a single question per hypothesis was not enough to adequately address the theory.

2.5.3 Data Collection Procedures

The professor at the college explained the survey items and then gave the survey to each student. When the students completed the survey, all surveys were placed in an envelope that was given to the researcher. The envelope was sealed to protect student confidentiality. Surveys are to remain anonymous so that each student will feel free to answer honestly without fear of reprisal. The surveys will be mailed to the researcher after they have been administered.

2.5.4 Data Coding

The conceptual variables are be (1) the perceived level of difficulty to pirate software, (2) the perceived harm pirating software causes, (3) software cost, (4) threat of punishment, and (5) the perceived right to use software without paying for it.

When the perceived level of difficulty to pirate software is operationalized it becomes the technical skill required to copy software, amount of time needed to copy software, and relative ease of copying software. Operationalizing the perceived harm pirating software causes makes it the perceived financial loss of companies from software piracy. The variable of software cost stays the same when operationalized meaning that it is already operationalized. The threat of punishment is operationalized into the likelihood of being caught and the perceived level of enforcement of copyright protection laws. The perceived right to use software without paying for it is operationalized into it is wrong to pirate software and software should be free.

If a survey contains missing data the survey will be discarded and none of the answers will be recorded.

2.5.5 Data Collected

Below is a dummy table containing the variables being measured and the possible responses for each one. The responses use the likert scale with a possible answer of strongly agree, agree, neutral, disagree, and strongly disagree. Below is a possible response from someone surveyed. They have marked their choice for each of the five questions by placing an X in the box associated with the scale of how much they agree or disagree with the statement.

Table 1. *Dummy Table of Responses*

Variable being Measured	Respondent Selections				
	Strongly Disagree	Disagree	Neutral	Agree	Strongly Agree
Difficulty of pirating software		X			
Impact of pirating software				X	
Expense of software			X		
Risk of being caught				X	
Morality of pirating sdftware				X	

9

2.5.6 Data Quality Assessment

A pilot study was issued to students at the Cleveland campus of the college, a career school offering associate degrees, and employees at the researcher's company, JurInnov, Ltd., a Cleveland based legal technology company.

A professor at the local college distributed this survey to his class on June 3, 2009. Three of those students and the teacher came to JurInnov on June 4, 2009 for a tour and time was spent discussing the survey with them. Additionally, four co-workers in the IT department at JurInnov were surveyed. The college class was chosen because it fits the population of students. Three of the eight students in the class attended a tour at JurInnov and their experience taking the survey was discussed. The four Information Technology (IT) workers were chosen because the researcher had direct access to them. The purpose of surveying the IT workers was to gain experience distributing a survey and to discuss that experience in this document.

Distributing a survey at work can be a difficult thing but JurInnov is a small company with only 20 employees. There are six people in IT. One was absent the day the survey was administered and the sixth person is Eric Vanderburg who manages the department so the survey was given to four employees. The IT team is a close-knit group. They have spent many hours together both inside and outside of work. There is a lot of trust and honesty between the team members. The surveys were put in the manager's drop box. The intent was to let the surveys remain anonymous. With a small group, handwriting could be an identifying factor so the IT team filled the survey out on a computer and then printed the forms. This way all forms look alike and they remained anonymous. The demographic questions were not asked of the IT team also because they could undermine the anonymity of the survey and the disclosure of salary information could be an issue for some employees.

When the survey was administered the survey items were each explained to the participant at JurInnov and then the employee was given time to complete the survey on the computer in private. When they had completed the survey they were asked to talk about their experience. The professor at the college explained the survey items and then gave the survey to each student. When the students completed the survey, all surveys were placed in an envelope that was given to the researcher on June 4, 2009.

The employees thought it was fun. Each person was talked to individually after they had completed the survey and the response was positive. Two individuals thought it was a joke because the topic was so far from what normally was discussed in the

workplace and their manager is known for jokes. They said they filled the survey out honestly but they thought that it was being collected for amusement. The students did not find the survey interesting and they took it because their teacher gave it to them. When asked about it they did not have many comments. Responses to the question "What did you think of the survey on software piracy?" included comments like "It was fine". Other questions resulted in similar responses. The feedback on the survey itself might have been better if it was solicited immediately after the survey was taken, as the survey items would have been fresh in the student's memories. None of the students reported any difficulty understanding the questions.

In a group discussion it seemed that perceptions of what is ok to do at home differ from what is ok to do at work. Questions 4 could be written in two ways, one for home and one for work. For example, Question 4a could be "Businesses have a right to use software without paying for it" and Question 4b could be "I have a right to use software without paying for it as long as it is for personal use". However, this could be more of an issue for working professionals, especially those in IT, rather than students so the survey for students could be fine as is.

The pilot test identified some things that could have been done differently including administering the survey to the students in person, discussing the survey immediately after administering the survey, and surveying a larger group of people.

Chapter 3

Results and Findings

3.1 Data Analysis

The purpose of this section is to analyze the data collected on software piracy. First the analysis procedures will be discussed and then the method of analysis will be explained. An explanation of the data will follow.

3.1.1 Analysis Procedures

The data was collected using a paper survey given to the students in their normal class period on June 17, 2009. This was the second survey some of the students received since some were part of the pilot test. The second survey that was distributed contained additional questions. They were given clear instructions on how to fill out the survey and then the completed surveys were collected by having the students drop them in a box in the front of the classroom.

3.1.2 Methods of Analysis

The variables were measured using a likert scale on a scale of 1 to 5 with a possible answer of strongly agree, agree, neutral, disagree, and strongly disagree.

The demographic variables were analyzed by computing the distribution across each category. Demographic variables include ethnicity, gender, income, financial aid, technical proficiency, student status, and risk tolerance. A quantitative approach was used to test the hypotheses of difficulty, impact, cost, risk, and right. The quantitative approach is used with the scaled variables. The Statistical Package for Social Science (SPSS) version 17 was used for hypothesis testing and to produce relevant demographic statistics.

3.2 Results

The variable names used are prefixed with H and then the number of the hypothesis they relate to. For example, H1Skill relates to hypothesis 1.

There were three ethnicities present in the study; White/Caucasian, Black/African American, and Hispanic. There were almost the same number of Black and White students, six Black (33.3%) and seven White (38.9%) and Hispanics made up the minority with four students (22.2%). The population did not contain Asian or Native American students. See table 1 for a summary of demographic variables pertaining to the study.

Table 2. *Ethnicity Distribution*

Ethnicity Distribution

		Frequency	Percent	Valid Percent	Cumulative Percent
Valid		1	5.6	5.6	5.6
	Black	6	33.3	33.3	38.9
	Hispanic	4	22.2	22.2	61.1
	White	7	38.9	38.9	100.0
	Total	18	100.0	100.0	

Figure 1: Ethnicity Distribution Pie Chart

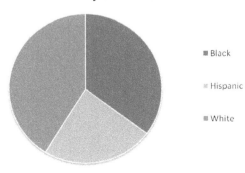

Ethnicity Distribution

■ Black

▨ Hispanic

■ White

13

Almost all students were male. Of the 17 students surveyed, 15 (83.3%) were male and two (11.1%) were female. Gharibyan and Gunsaulus state, "It is well known that women's involvement in the field of Computer Science is very low in the USA" (2006, p. 222). Akbulut et al. found that male students were more likely than female students to take unethical actions. They also found that the tendency of a female student to take unethical actions was not influenced by their declared major but it was for men (2008). This study can build on the work of Akbulut et al. by comparing the proclivity towards unethical behavior in male and female students who have declared a computer major. See table 2 for additional information on gender distribution.

Table 3. *Gender Distribution*

Gender Distribution

		Frequency	Percent	Valid Percent	Cumulative Percent
Valid		1	5.6	5.6	5.6
	Female	2	11.1	11.1	16.7
	Male	15	83.3	83.3	100.0
	Total	18	100.0	100.0	

Income distributions represented only the lower three portions of the scale with no one earning more than $50,000. The question listed six categories; Less than $10,000, $10,001 - $25,000, $25,001 - $50,000, $50,001 - $75,000, $75,001 - $100,000, and More than $100,000. See table 3 for the details. The upper three categories are not listed in the table because there were no students who fit into those categories.

This could be related to the student status since all students reported a status of full-time. If students are taking a full load of classes they might not be able to work many hours so they would earn less than average. Another variable that was not studied was age. Younger students who come directly out of high school may not have worked yet and so they would fall into the $10,000 or less category. Since this demographic information was not collected, no conclusions can be made on why the population fell into the lower three income categories. Income and financial aid information was obtained because the economic means of a person has been related to the tendency to pirate software. Marron and Steel (2000) found economic means to be inversely related

to software piracy. Additionally, Depken and Simmons (2004) concluded that software piracy declines as income increases.

Table 4. *Income Distribution*

Income Distribution

		Frequency	Percent	Valid Percent	Cumulative Percent
Valid	$Less than $10,000	5	27.8	29.4	29.4
	$$10,001 - $25,000	5	27.8	29.4	58.8
	$$25,001 - $50,000	7	38.9	41.2	100.0
	Total	17	94.4	100.0	
Missing	System	1	5.6		
Total		18	100.0		

All students were on financial aid. The question was a yes or no question which all students answered yes to indicating that they were receiving financial aid. The school does a good job helping the students obtain financial aid and they all have taken advantage of the opportunity. See table 4 for the details.

Table 5. *Financial Aid Distribution*

Financial Aid Distribution

		Frequency	Percent	Valid Percent	Cumulative Percent
Valid		1	5.6	5.6	5.6
	Yes	17	94.4	94.4	100.0
	Total	18	100.0	100.0	

The next demographic variable recorded was technical proficiency which is the ability one has in technical areas such as computing and information systems. Students could select one of five levels for this question; very proficient, above average, average, below average, and not proficient. The students all answered that they were at minimum average in technical proficiency with six (33.3%) stating that they were above average and five (27.8%) stating that they were very proficient. Since all the students

were in the computer technology program it makes sense that they would consider themselves average or above. It actually is of note that one third of the students only considered themselves average and not above average. Technological proficiency is an important demographic variable that has been studied previously by Gan and Koh in 2006. Gan and Koh's study found that those with 8-10 years of personal computer experience tended to pirate software seldom whereas those with 4 or less years experience with personal computers pirated often. See table 5 for the details.

Table 6. *Technical Proficiency Distribution*

Technical Proficiency Distribution

		Frequency	Percent	Valid Percent	Cumulative Percent
Valid	Very Proficient	5	27.8	29.4	29.4
	Above Average	6	33.3	35.3	64.7
	Average	6	33.3	35.3	100.0
	Total	17	94.4	100.0	
Missing	System	1	5.6		
Total		18	100.0		

All students were full-time students. This means that they take a full credit load of at least 12 credit hours. The information is depicted in table 6.

Table 7. *Student Status Distribution*

Student Status Distribution

	Frequency	Percent	Valid Percent	Cumulative Percent
Valid	1	5.6	5.6	5.6
Full Time	17	94.4	94.4	100.0
Total	18	100.0	100.0	

The last demographic variable that was measured was risk tolerance. The students ranked themselves on a scale of low, below average, average, above average, and high. The distribution was even above and below average. Only one student

admitted to being a high risk taker and only one listed themselves as a low risk taker. Half of the students answered that they were average risk takers. An equal number (16.7%) answered either below average or above average. The data is presented in table 7.

Table 8. *Risk Distribution*

Risk Distribution

		Frequency	Percent	Valid Percent	Cumulative Percent
Valid	High	1	5.6	5.9	5.9
	Above Average	3	16.7	17.6	23.5
	Average	9	50.0	52.9	76.5
	Below Average	3	16.7	17.6	94.1
	Low	1	5.6	5.9	100.0
	Total	17	94.4	100.0	
Missing	System	1	5.6		
Total		18	100.0		

Two t-tests were conducted. The first t-test was conducted on the data where the respondents answered yes to the question "Would you pirate software?" and the second tested the cases where respondents answered no.

Here are the results from the yes cases. These students said that they would pirate software. H1Skill, H1Ease, and H1Speed are all negatively correlated with the hypothesis 1 stating that the likelihood of a student choosing to pirate software is independent of the perceived level of difficulty. H1Skill states that copying software does not require a lot of technical skill. H1Ease states it is simple to copy software. H1Speed states the process of copying software is quick. The mean of H1Skill was 3.36, the mean of H1Ease was 3.21, and the mean of H1Speed was 3.29. On the likert scale these values fall in between neutral and agree. The values are not high enough to reject the null hypothesis.

H2Impact is negatively correlated with hypothesis 2 stating that the likelihood of a student choosing to pirate software is independent of the perceived harm pirating software causes. H2Impact states pirating software is harmless. H2Loss is positively correlated with hypothesis 2. H2Loss states software companies lose money when I copy software.

H2Impact had a mean value of 3.07 which is not high enough to reject the null hypothesis. H2Loss had a mean value of 2.64 which would map to an average selection of disagree to the question; software companies lose money when I copy software. However, 2.64 is closer to 3 (neutral) than it is to 2 (disagree) so it does not provide evidence to support the null hypothesis.

H3Cost and H3Value are negatively correlated with hypothesis 3 stating the likelihood of a student choosing to pirate software is independent of the software cost. H3Cost states that software is too expensive. H3Cost has a mean of 3.93 and H3Value has a mean of 3.57. H3Valuie states software is not worth the price companies charge for it. Neither of these values is high enough to reject the null hypothesis.

H4Risk and H4Law are negatively correlated with hypothesis 4 stating the likelihood of a student choosing to pirate software is independent of the threat of punishment. H4Risk states that it is doubtful that I would be caught if I pirated software. H4Risk had a mean of 3.64 and H4Law had a mean of 3.36. H4Law states that copyright protection laws are not often enforced. Neither of these values is high enough to reject the null hypothesis.

H5Right is negatively correlated with hypothesis 5 stating The likelihood of a student choosing to pirate software is independent of the perceived right to use the software without paying for it. H5Moral is positively correlated with hypothesis 5 and H5Intangible is negatively correlated with hypothesis 5. H5Right states I have a right to use software without paying for it. H5Right had a mean of 3.00 which is completely neutral. This value is not sufficient to provide evidence to support the null hypothesis. H5Moral states that it is wrong to pirate software. H5Moral had a mean of 2.50. This value is not high enough to reject the null hypothesis. It shows that on average those who pirate software disagree with the statement, it is wrong to pirate software. H5Intangible states that software is intangible and should not be paid for. H5Intangible had a mean of 3.00. Similar to H5Right, 3.00 is not sufficient to provide evidence to support the null hypothesis.

The analysis shows that those who answered yes had a mean income of $28,571, a mean technical skill of 2.143 which maps to above average technical proficiency. Please see table 9 for the complete results of the one sample t test for those who do pirate software.

Table 9. *One-Sample Test for Yes Respondents*

One-Sample Test for Yes respondents

	Test Value = 0					
					95% Confidence Interval of the Difference	
	t	df	Sig. (2-tailed)	Mean Difference	Lower	Upper
H1Skill	12.459	13	.000	3.357	2.78	3.94
H1Ease	10.121	13	.000	3.214	2.53	3.90
H1Speed	11.500	13	.000	3.286	2.67	3.90
H2Impact	10.071	13	.000	3.071	2.41	3.73
H2Loss	10.647	13	.000	2.643	2.11	3.18
H3Cost	20.135	13	.000	3.929	3.51	4.35
H3Value	14.252	13	.000	3.571	3.03	4.11
H4Risk	18.297	13	.000	3.643	3.21	4.07
H4Laws	14.920	13	.000	3.357	2.87	3.84
H5Right	11.683	13	.000	3.000	2.45	3.55
H5Moral	9.946	13	.000	2.500	1.96	3.04
H5Intangible	10.817	13	.000	3.000	2.40	3.60
DemIncome	6.041	13	.000	$28,571.429	$18,353.44	$38,789.42
DemTech	9.275	13	.000	2.143	1.64	2.64

Here are the results from the no cases. These students said that they would not pirate software. H1Skill had a mean of 4.333 which is means that on average these students agreed that copying software does not require a lot of technical skill. H1Ease also had a mean of 4.333 meaning that on average the students agreed that it is simple to copy software. For H1Speed the mean was 3.667 which falls in between neutral and agree.

H2Impact and H2Loss both had means of 3.000 which maps to neutral answers to whether pirating software is harmless and whether software companies lose money when software is pirated.

H3Cost had a mean of 3.333 which shows that respondents were neutral to the question of software being too expensive. H3Value, however, had a mean of 4.000 which means that the students on average agreed with the statement that software is not worth the price companies charge for it.

H4Risk had a mean of 2.667 which means that students are neutral or disagree to the question, it is doubtful that I would be caught if I pirated software. They are either unsure as to whether pirating software is risky or they perceive a risk. H4Laws had a mean of 2.667 as well which means that students are neutral or disagree to the question, copyright protection laws are often not enforced. This means that they are either unsure or they believe that laws are enforced.

H5Right had a mean of 1.667 falling between strongly disagree and disagree to the question I have a right to use software without paying for it. This means that the students who would not copy software believe that they should not copy software. H5Moral had a mean of 4.000 meaning that the students on average agreed that it is wrong to pirate software. H5Intangible had a mean of 1.6667 which means that the students either strongly disagree or disagree with the statement, software is intangible and should not be paid for.

The mean income of the students who would not copy software was $41,666 and they believed themselves to be either very proficient or above average with technology. Please see table 10 for the complete results of the one-sample t test for those who do not pirate software.

Table 10. *One-Sample Test for No Respondents*

One-Sample Test for No respondents

| | Test Value = 0 | | | | | |
| | t | df | Sig. (2-tailed) | Mean Difference | 95% Confidence Interval of the Difference | |
					Lower	Upper
H1Skill	13.000	2	.006	4.333	2.90	5.77
H1Ease	13.000	2	.006	4.333	2.90	5.77
H1Speed	11.000	2	.008	3.667	2.23	5.10
H2Impact	5.196	2	.035	3.000	.52	5.48
H2Loss	3.000	2	.095	3.000	-1.30	7.30
H3Cost	3.780	2	.063	3.333	-.46	7.13
H3Value	6.928	2	.020	4.000	1.52	6.48
H4Risk	8.000	2	.015	2.667	1.23	4.10
H4Laws	4.000	2	.057	2.667	-.20	5.54
H5Right	2.500	2	.130	1.667	-1.20	4.54
H5Moral	6.928	2	.020	4.000	1.52	6.48
H5Intangible	5.000	2	.038	1.667	.23	3.10
DemIncome	5.000	2	.038	$41,666.667	$5,811.23	$77,522.11
DemTech	5.000	2	.038	1.667	.23	3.10

3.3 Findings

There is a definite difference between the students who pirate software and those who do not. Those who would not copy software earned on average 45.8% more than those who would copy software. These students also believed that it is wrong to pirate software and they believed that software should be paid for. The students who do pirate software did not believe that it is wrong to copy software but they were neutral as to whether or not they have a right to use software without paying for it.

Those who do not pirate software believed it simpler to copy software than those who do copy it and they also believed that it required less technical skill. They also were slightly more inclined to believe that they would be caught if they pirated software. Please refer to table 11 for a side-by-side comparison of the means between those who pirate software and those who do not.

Table 11. *Comparison of Mean Responses base on Yes or No Response*

Question	Does pirate software	Does not pirate software
Copying software does not require a lot of technical skill.	3.357	4.333
It is simple to copy software.	3.214	4.333
The process of copying software is quick.	3.286	3.667
Pirating software is harmless	3.071	3.000
Software companies lose money when I copy software.	2.643	3.000
Software is too expensive	3.929	3.333
Software is not worth the price companies charge for it.	3.571	4.000
It is doubtful that I would be caught if I pirated software	3.643	2.667
Copyright protection laws are not often enforced.	3.357	2.667
I have a right to use software without paying for it	3.000	1.667
It is wrong to pirate software.	2.500	4.000
Software is intangible and should not be paid for.	3.000	1.667

22

Chapter 4

Implications and Conclusions

4.1 Contributions to Knowledge

The results of this study show that students who pirate software do not believe it to be wrong while those who do not pirate software believed it to be wrong and they believed that they do not have a right to use the software without paying for it. This knowledge will aid in computer ethics education because it shows that the beliefs and moral attitudes of the students in computer technology programs are consistent with their actions to pirate software.

This research extends previous work enhancing knowledge of the subject. This study takes place two years after the work of Siponen and Vartiainen and it will assist in determining trends in reasons for piracy among college students.

4.2 Implications for Future Research

Some items for future studies include comparing students with work experience to those without work experience. Are students with work experience less likely to pirate software? Do students with work experience ascribe more importance to software copyright laws? Age would also be an important area for future study. Are younger students more likely to copy software illegally? Another question for further research would be, are students less inclined to pirate software as they matriculate?

4.3 Implications for Practitioners

Software companies need to be able to make a profit from their work. In order to protect their intellectual property they need to understand why software is pirated. Software piracy is often mentioned in the media but the reasons for why people copy software are largely unknown (Siponen and Vartiainen, 2007). This research builds on that of Siponen and Vartiainen by surveying students in the United States who are preparing to work in the computer industry.

4.4 Implications for Policy Makers

This research is helpful for policy makers because they are concerned with adherence to software licensing agreements and upholding the law. If it is better understood why software is pirated among students, college administrators can design better policies to curb this behavior.

4.5 Conclusions

The goal of this study was to analyze the factors contributing to a student's decision to pirate software. The study focused on students in computer technology disciplines. It builds on the work of Siponen and Vartiainen (2007), Gan and Koh (2006), Depken and Simmons (2004), Marron and Steel (2000), Kin-wai Lau (2007), and Vitell and Davis (1990) who studied software piracy and Akbulut (2008) who studied ethics between genders. The results of the study show that the moral attitudes of whether it is wrong to pirate software are present in those who do not copy software but absent in those who do. The research is valuable for IA (Information Assurance) practitioners and policy makers.

APPENDICES

Appendix A
Definition of Terms

Software Piracy : The unauthorized and unlawful reproduction, distribution, or modification of software.

Technological Proficiency : The aptitude and skill in computers and information technology.

Appendix B

List of Symbols and Acronyms

IT: Information Technology

SPSS: Statistical Package for Social Science

IA: Information Assurance

Appendix C

Instrument(s) Utilized

C.1 Pilot Test Instrument

Demographic Information

For each question below, please select only one answer by checking the appropriate box.

What is your ethnicity?

- o Caucasian/White
- o African-American/Black
- o Hispanic
- o Asian/Pacific Islander
- o Native American
- o Other

What is your gender?

- o Male
- o Female

What is your household income?

- o Less than $10,000
- o $10,001 - $25,000
- o $25,001 - $50,000
- o $50,001 - $75,000
- o $75,001 - $100,000
- o More than $100,000

Are you on Financial Aid?

- o Yes
- o No

How would you rate your technological proficiency?

- o Very Proficient
- o Above Average
- o Average

c Below Average

o Not Proficient

What is your student status?

    o Full Time

    o Part Time

What is your tolerance of risk?

    o High

    ɔ Above Average

    ɔ Average

    o Below Average

    o Low

Thank you for participating in this survey on software piracy. We greatly appreciate your response. All information collected will be kept strictly confidential. Information collected here will only be published in aggregate. If you have any questions, please ask the person administering this survey and they will be happy to help.

Please answer the following questions by circling the appropriate number. 1 stands for strongly disagree, 2 for disagree, 3 for neutral, 4 for agree, and 5 for strongly agree. Please answer all questions and provide only one answer for each question. Incomplete surveys and those with multiple answers will be discarded. Please fold this paper in half and drop it in the box at the front of the room.

Question	Strongly Disagree	Disagree	Neutral	Agree	Strongly Agree
Pirating software is easy to do	1	2	3	4	5
Pirating software is harmless	1	2	3	4	5
Software is too expensive	1	2	3	4	5
It is doubtful that I would be caught if I pirated software	1	2	3	4	5
I have a right to use software without paying for it	1	2	3	4	5
I would pirate software	1	2	3	4	5

C.2 Data Collection Instrument

Demographic Information

For each question below, please select only one answer by checking the appropriate box.

What is your ethnicity?

- o Caucasian/White
- o African-American/Black
- o Hispanic
- o Asian/Pacific Islander
- o Native American
- o Other

What is your gender?

- o Male
- o Female

What is your household income?

- o Less than $10,000
- o $10,001 - $25,000
- o $25,001 - $50,000
- o $50,001 - $75,000
- o $75,001 - $100,000
- o More than $100,000

Are you on Financial Aid?

- o Yes
- o No

How would you rate your technological proficiency?

- o Very Proficient
- o Above Average
- o Average

- o Below Average
- o Not Proficient

What is your student status?

- o Full Time
- o Part Time

What is your tolerance of risk?

- o High
- o Above Average
- o Average
- o Below Average
- o Low

Instructions:

Thank you for participating in this survey on software piracy. We greatly appreciate your response. All information collected will be kept strictly confidential. Information collected here will only be published in aggregate. If you have any questions, please ask the person administering this survey and they will be happy to help. When you have completed the survey, please fold this paper in half and drop it in the box at the front of the room.

Software piracy is the illegal duplication and/or distribution of copyrighted software. It can take the form of copying software media, copying software over a network, downloading software illegally, tampering with software to remove copy protections or authentication methods, hosting illegal software for download, and installing software on more machines than a license permits.

Item No.	Please answer the following questions by circling the appropriate number. 1 stands for strongly disagree, 2 for disagree, 3 for neutral, 4 for agree, and 5 for strongly agree. Please answer all questions and provide only one answer for each question. Incomplete surveys and those with multiple answers will be discarded.	Strongly Disagree	Disagree	Neutral	Agree	Strongly Agree
1	Copying software does not require a lot of technical skill.	1	2	3	4	5
2	It is simple to copy software.	1	2	3	4	5
3	The process of copying software is quick.	1	2	3	4	5
4	Pirating software is harmless	1	2	3	4	5
5	Software companies lose money when I copy software.	1	2	3	4	5
6	Software is too expensive	1	2	3	4	5
7	Software is not worth the price companies charge for it.	1	2	3	4	5
8	It is doubtful that I would be caught if I pirated software	1	2	3	4	5
9	Copyright protection laws are not often enforced.	1	2	3	4	5
10	I have a right to use software without paying for it	1	2	3	4	5
11	It is wrong to pirate software.	1	2	3	4	5
12	Software is intangible and should not be paid for.	1	2	3	4	5
Answer the next question with Yes or No						
13	Would you pirate software?	Yes			No	

Reference List

Akbulut, Y., Uysal, &., mer, ., Odabasi, H. F., & Kuzu, A. (2008). Influence of gender, program of study and PC experience on unethical computer using behaviors of Turkish undergraduate students. Computers & Education, 51(2), 485-492.

Depken II, C.A., Simmons, L., (2004). Social construct and the propensity for software piracy, with Lee C. Simmons. Applied Economics Letters 11, 97 – 100.

Gan, L. L, & Koh, H. C. (2006). An empirical study of software piracy among tertiary institutions in Singapore. *Information & Management.* 43(5), 640-649.

Gharibyan, H., & Gunsaulus, S. (2006). Gender Gap in Computer Science Does Not Exist in Former Soviet Republic: Results of a Study. Proceedings of the 11th annual SIGCSE conference on Innovation and technology in computer science education. Bologna: Italy

Kin-wai Lau, E. (2007). Interaction effects in software piracy. *Business Ethics: A European Review*, 16(1), 34-47.

Marron, D.B., & Steel, D.G., (2000). Which countries protect intellectual property? The case of software piracy. *Economic Inquiry* 38, 159-174.

Punch, K.F. (2005). *Introduction to social research: Quantitative and qualitative approaches (2nd Ed.).* London: Sage Publications.

Siponen, M. T., Vartiainen, T. (2007). Unauthorized copying of software – An empirical study of reasons for and against. *SIGCAS Computers and Society*, 37(1), 30-43.

Vitell, S, J., & Davis, D. L. (1990). Ethical beliefs of MIS professionals: The frequency and opportunity for unethical behavior. Journal of Business Ethics. 9(1), 63-70.

www.ingramcontent.com/pod-product-compliance
Lightning Source LLC
Chambersburg PA
CBHW031228050326
40689CB00009B/1517